LEONARDO DA VINCI

DIANE STANLEY

MORROW JUNIOR BOOKS

New York

for Peter

The author would like to thank Professor John Shearman of the
Harvard University Department of Fine Arts for his helpful reading of the text.

The drawings on the text pages are from Leonardo's notebooks. The knotted borders were adapted from a design by Leonardo.

PRONUNCIATION GUIDE

Albiera di Giovanni Amadori	ahl-bee-*yer*-uh dee jee-oh-*vahn*-ee ah-mah-*doh*-ree
Amboise	ahm-*bwahs*
Andrea del Verrocchio	ahn-*dray*-ah del vuh-*roh*-kee-oh
Anghiari	*ahn*-gee-*ahr*-ee
Cascina	kah-*shee*-nah
Cesare Borgia	*chay*-zah-ray *bore*-jhuh
chiaroscuro	kee-*ahr*-uh-*skew*-roh
Cloux	*cloo*
contrapposto	*kohn*-trah-*post*-oh
Francesco Melzi	frahn-*ches*-koh *melts*-ee
Leonardo da Vinci	*lay*-uh-*nar*-doh dah *vin*-chee
Lorenzo de' Medici	loh-*ren*-zoh day *may*-dee-chee
Ludovico Sforza	loo-doh-*vee*-koh *sfort*-suh
Michelangelo Buonarroti	*my*-kul-*an*-jel-oh *bwohn*-uh-*roh*-tee
Niccolò Machiavelli	nee-koh-*loh* mahk-ee-uh-*vel*-lee
Palazzo della Signoria	puh-*lah*-tzoh day-lah *seen*-yoh-*ree*-ah
Renaissance	*ren*-ih-sans
Saint-Florentin	sahnt *floh*-ren-teen
Salai	*sah*-lah-ee
Santa Maria delle Grazie	*sahn*-tah mah-*ree*-ah day-lay *grah*-tzee-ay
Ser Giuliano	*sehr* joo-lee-*ah*-noh
Ser Piero	*sehr* pee-*yer*-roh

Manufactured in Hong Kong by South China Printing Company Ltd.   16 17 18 19 20
The art was prepared using watercolor, gouache, colored pencil, and photo collage on Whatman watercolor paper. The text type is 13.5-point Bernhard Modern BT.

Library of Congress Cataloging-in-Publication Data   Stanley, Diane.   Leonardo da Vinci/by Diane Stanley.   p. cm.   Includes bibliographical references.
Summary: A biography of the Italian Renaissance artist and inventor who, at about age thirty, began writing his famous notebooks, which contain the outpourings of his amazing mind.
ISBN 0-688-10437-1 (trade)—ISBN 0-688-10438-X (library)
ISBN 0-688-16155-3 (paper back)
1. Leonardo, da Vinci, 1452–1519—Criticism and interpretation—Juvenile literature.   [1. Leonardo, da Vinci, 1452–1519.   2. Artists.]
I. Title.   N6923.L33S72 1996   709'.2—dc20   [B]   95-35227   CIP AC

The author would like to acknowledge the following sources: Giraudon/Art Resource, New York,
Virgin and Child with St. Anne; Erich Lessing/Art Resource, New York, *The Adoration of the Magi* (unfinished);
Scala/Art Resource, New York, *Mona Lisa, The Virgin of the Rocks, The Last Supper.*

Leonardo da Vinci lived in exciting times. A thousand years had passed since the Roman Empire fell, a thousand years in which the people of Europe tended their farms, went to war, and guided every act by a deep religious faith. In the Middle Ages few besides priests could read, and books were rare treasures copied by hand.

Then, at about the time Leonardo was born, things began to change. Faith and tradition gave way to learning and curiosity. Explorers such as Vasco da Gama, Christopher Columbus, and Ferdinand Magellan sailed off on voyages of discovery. A growing class of merchants grew rich on trade, and more and more people left the countryside and went to work in cities. There they could buy books, thanks to Johann Gutenberg and his new printing press. Now ordinary people could read the great works of the ancient Greeks and Romans. As they became more educated, they started thinking for themselves and questioning old ideas, as Nicolaus Copernicus did when he suggested that the earth was not the center of the universe. It was an age of great accomplishments, and one of its true glories was the birth of a new kind of art.

The most exciting place to be in those exciting times was Italy, where the new age began. The sunny peninsula shaped like a boot was not a unified country then. Though the whole area was often called Italy, it really consisted of a number of independent states. The most powerful were the Republic of Venice, the Duchy of Milan, the Kingdom of Naples, the Papal States (Rome), and the Republic of Florence. It was Florence—the richest state, though not the biggest—that was the center of this artistic revolution. It was there that Brunelleschi worked out the science of perspective, Michelangelo sculpted the *David,* and Leonardo painted the *Mona Lisa.*

So many brilliant artists had arisen in Italy since the thirteenth century that a man by the name of Giorgio Vasari decided to write a book about them. When he published his *Lives of the Most Eminent Painters, Sculptors, and Architects,* in 1550, he became the first art historian. At the same time, he also gave a name to that exceptional period in history. He called it a rebirth. We still use that word today, in its French form. We call it the Renaissance.

In the spring of 1452 Antonio da Vinci, aged eighty, took out a leather-bound volume. In it were recorded all the important events in the life of his family, going back to his grand-father's time. Antonio opened the book to the last page. He had not written anything in it for sixteen years, and he saw that there was room at the bottom for only one more entry. This is what he wrote:

1452
There was born to me a grandson, son of Ser Piero my son, on 15 April, a Saturday,
at the third hour of the night. He bears the name Leonardo.

Antonio then wrote about the priest who had baptized the child and all the witnesses present for the occasion. But there was one person he did not mention—Leonardo's mother.

Her name was Caterina, and she was a peasant. Though Ser Piero may have been very fond of Caterina, he did not marry her. After all, he was an important man, a leading citizen of Vinci. Like his grandfather and great-grandfather before him, he had studied at the university to become a notary, someone who prepared contracts and other legal documents. He expected to marry a young woman with money who came from a good family, someone just like him. And indeed, a few months later Ser Piero married just such a girl, the sixteen-year-old Albiera di Giovanni Amadori.

Leonardo probably lived with his mother at first. But a couple of years later Caterina also got married—to a man of her class who was known by the nickname the Quarreler. Perhaps this is when Leonardo moved in with his father.

We know that by the time he was five, Leonardo was living in his grandfather's house near the village of Vinci, twenty miles from Florence. Whether he was happy there is another question. His father, stern and businesslike, saved his affection for his young wife. And Albiera, who must have looked after Leonardo, died childless when he was only twelve. A year later the practical Ser Piero replaced her with a new wife who was not much older than Leonardo. She too would die—only eight years later—without children.

But fortunately for Leonardo, he found a loving friend in his young uncle Francesco. Antonio described Francesco as "my son who lives at home and does nothing." In fact, he ran the farm, where wheat and buckwheat grew; the vineyards, where grapes were cultivated to make wine; and the olive groves. He was a gentle and independent man, not ambitious like his older brother. It was probably with Francesco that Leonardo explored the countryside and began his lifelong fascination with nature.

Leonardo had a country childhood and a country education. What little schooling he got probably came from the parish priest and was limited to reading, writing, and simple arithmetic. He later described himself as an *omo sanza lettere,* a "man without education." Of course, if he had been legitimate—born to married parents—he would have been taught Latin and geometry and sent to the University of Florence. There he would probably have studied to be a notary, like his father. But because he was illegitimate, the guild of magistrates and notaries would not accept him. For the same reason he could not be a doctor or a pharmacist or a banker. He could not even attend the university. Ser Piero probably thought that education would be wasted on the boy.

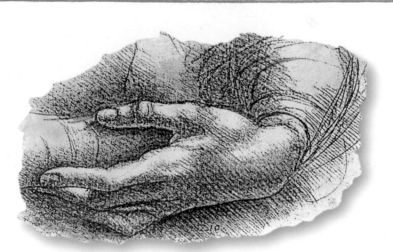

Since the noble professions were closed to Leonardo, he would have to do something else. The boy did show a definite talent for drawing. So Ser Piero took him to Florence and apprenticed him to the famous artist Andrea del Verrocchio. It turned out to be a happy choice. Not only was Verrocchio a great teacher, but he came to love and understand his remarkable pupil.

Leonardo moved into Verrocchio's workshop, where he was to live with the other apprentices for the next six to ten years. These were not boys from well-to-do families like Leonardo's. Artists were usually the sons of such tradesmen as butchers, tanners, or stonemasons.

At first, Leonardo helped out around the workshop by running errands and sweeping floors. Later he learned to grind colors and make brushes. But the apprentices were there to learn a trade, and Verrocchio made them practice drawing every day, often by copying plaster models of hands, feet, or drapery. When they mastered drawing, they moved on to painting in the new Flemish technique, in which powdered colors were mixed with oil instead of water. They also studied architecture and made sculptures in clay, bronze, and marble.

Besides all that, artists made patterns for tapestries and carpets, painted banners for festivals, and produced the sets and costumes for pageants. They weren't expected to develop individual styles, as artists do today. At that time they were thought of as mere craftsmen who worked for hire. They never even signed their paintings, which were often the combined efforts of the master and his older apprentices.

There is a story that when Leonardo had been studying with Verrocchio for quite some time, he helped paint a picture of St. John baptizing Jesus. Verrocchio had already finished most of it. Leonardo painted one of the angels and completed the background. It is said that when Verrocchio saw Leonardo's angel, he was struck by how much finer it was than anything else in the picture—and never picked up a paintbrush again.

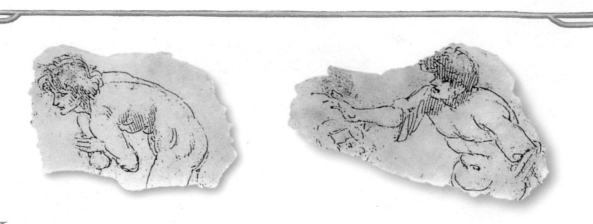

When Leonardo was twenty, he was accepted into the painters' guild. But his career got off to a very slow start. As he was to do all his life, he began projects only to abandon them. No one is sure why. It may be that his true interests lay elsewhere and that the long and meticulous process of painting bored him.

He obviously enjoyed the first part, when he sketched and planned the composition of the picture, often lingering over this stage for months. Then he would move on to the next step— making the cartoon. Today we think of a cartoon as a comic line drawing, but in Leonardo's time the word meant the finished sketch from which a painting was made. The cartoon was drawn the same size as the picture was to be, so Leonardo sometimes had to glue many small sheets of paper together to make a sheet large enough for his design. When the cartoon was finished, he attached it to the wooden panel or wall on which he was going to paint. Following the outlines, he punched little holes in the paper. Finally he pressed black chalk through the holes onto the panel or wall. When the paper was removed, the picture had been transferred and was ready to paint.

Next came the underpainting. Here he laid down all the shadows and modeling that made the picture look three-dimensional. This was usually done in neutral earth tones, such as brown or gray. Only after the underpainting was complete did he begin to add the color, patiently laying down many delicate layers of oil paint.

Leonardo had reached the underpainting stage of a large altarpiece, *The Adoration of the Magi,* when he simply abandoned it. Perhaps the project had grown tedious and he longed for the varied tasks and good pay a great patron could offer him. In Florence the obvious patron was Lorenzo de' Medici, who ruled the city. Known as Lorenzo the Magnificent, he was fabulously rich, an intellectual, and a lover of poetry and music. Unfortunately, though his city was famed for its brilliant painters, he put few of them to work. So Leonardo left Florence, at about the age of thirty, and headed north, for Milan.

The Duchy of Milan was ruled by Duke Ludovico Sforza. Like Lorenzo the Magnificent, he was known by a nickname—because of his black hair and dark skin, the duke was called the Moor, after the Arabs of North Africa. But he was quite different from the cultured Lorenzo. The Moor was an arrogant and ambitious man who gambled at war and lived lavishly in peace. He did share one trait with his fellow ruler—a love of music. According to Vasari, it was music, and not art, that first brought Leonardo to the court of the Moor.

Leonardo was said to have had a beautiful singing voice and great skill at playing the *lira da braccio,* an early instrument much like the modern violin. He even designed musical instruments, including a bizarre silver *lira* in the shape of a horse's skull that he supposedly made as a gift for the Moor. He might even have entertained the court by playing and singing. But he did not plan to work as a musician. When he had given a lot of thought to what skills he had to offer, he composed an extraordinary letter to the Moor. Though we have only an unsigned rough draft, scholars agree that it is genuine.

He began by calling the duke "Most Illustrious Lord," then got right to the point. Leonardo claimed that he had studied all the latest "machines of war" and had come up with many improvements and some secret new ideas. He listed nine of them, beginning with "very strong but light bridges, extremely easy to carry." He claimed to be able to "dry up the water of the moats" during sieges, destroy fortresses, and dig tunnels under walls and even under rivers. He had designs for bombards, mortars, catapults, covered assault vehicles, and weapons for battles at sea.

Near the end of the letter he added that he was a master of architecture and that he could build canals, make sculptures, and—almost as if it were an afterthought—paint "as well as any man, whoever he be."

We don't know what Ludovico thought of the letter, but it seems that he did not give Leonardo work right away. However, he may have recommended Leonardo for his first commission in Milan, to paint an altarpiece for the church of San Francesco Grande.

The monks there knew exactly what they wanted Leonardo to do, and they spelled it out in the contract. It was to be a picture of "Our Lady and her Son with the Angels, done in oil with the utmost care, and with these, two Prophets." Mary was to be dressed in a gown of gold brocade and deep blue, lined with green. The monks wanted God the Father looking down, and he was to wear blue and gold. The angels were to have golden halos, and Jesus was to be posed on a golden platform. What they wanted, in short, was a very traditional, old-fashioned kind of picture—stiff, formal, and unrealistic. Leonardo signed the contract, then proceeded to ignore everything in it.

The monks were to have no prophets, no God the Father, and only one angel. There was no throne and no gold leaf, not even in Mary's robe, which was blue, lined with yellow. The baby Jesus sat on the grass, wearing nothing at all. And as if to be completely contrary, Leonardo decided to add the infant St. John to his picture. Mary was a fresh-faced young girl sweetly introducing two plump babies to each other. And the angel, whose wings were lost in shadow, looked like a handsome young traveler who had just stopped to admire the children. But most shocking of all, none of them had a halo! No one had ever painted such a picture before.

The painting must have been the talk of Milan, but once people got used to this new kind of art, they admired it greatly. Best of all, Ludovico the Moor liked it too, and Leonardo finally had a patron.

Those were busy years. Leonardo was on call to do whatever his patron wanted—design a heating system for the duchess's bath, for example, or paint a portrait of the Moor's favorite lady. He oversaw the pouring of metal into molds for the making of cannons. He decorated the vaulted ceiling of a room in Ludovico's castle with a grove of trees, and he worked as an engineer in the building of canals. For special occasions he organized pageants and entertainments, supervising every detail from designing the costumes to choosing the music.

For the marriage of Ludovico's nephew to the granddaughter of the king of Naples, Ludovico wanted something spectacular. Since he was a great believer in astrology, the Moor decided on a "Masque of the Planets." What Leonardo created for his patron turned out to be so marvelous that it went down in history as the "Feast of Paradise."

The evening began with a lavish banquet, followed by music and dancing. All the guests wore costumes and masks, while the Moor was exotic in Oriental clothes. At midnight Ludovico stopped the music. The curtain rose, and the guests gazed at what Leonardo had made.

There on the stage before them was a scene of rugged mountains. As music began to play (covering the creaks and groans of the revolving stage), the mountain in the center opened to reveal a glittering dome. It was cleverly lit from behind so that it looked like the night sky sprinkled with stars. Surrounding this glorious sphere were the twelve signs of the zodiac, lit by torches. Handsome actors portrayed the seven heavenly bodies that could be seen in those days before the telescope. Beautifully dressed as the Sun, Moon, Mercury, Venus, Mars, Jupiter, and Saturn, they rotated gracefully in their mechanical orbits. While all this was going on, the three Graces and seven Virtues came onstage to give speeches in praise of the bride. One man who saw the spectacle wrote about it later. "So great was the splendor," he declared, "that one first believed they were seeing the real Paradise."

The world saw Leonardo as courtly and charming. But at heart he was a solitary man. "If you are alone," he once wrote, "you belong entirely to yourself.... If you are accompanied by even one companion you belong only half to yourself, or even less." In the peace of his aloneness, Leonardo could imagine, create, and dream. It is easy to picture him, then, in his room by himself, writing in one of his famous notebooks.

He began them when he was about thirty. Over the years he filled thousands of pages with the outpourings of his amazing mind. There were drawings of grotesque faces, drafts of letters, sketches for future paintings, lists of books he owned, plans for inventions, moral observations, pages copied out of books he had borrowed, notes of things to remember, designs for weapons, drawings of anatomy, and observations of nature. On one page, for example, you can find geometry problems, a plan for building canals, and the note "Tuesday: bread, meat, wine, fruit, vegetables, salad."

All this was written in a peculiar backward script, going from right to left. You must use a mirror to read it. This has led to the myth that he wrote that way to keep his notebooks safe from prying eyes. In fact, Leonardo was left-handed and found it much easier to write that way. When he *really* wanted to keep something secret, he wrote in code.

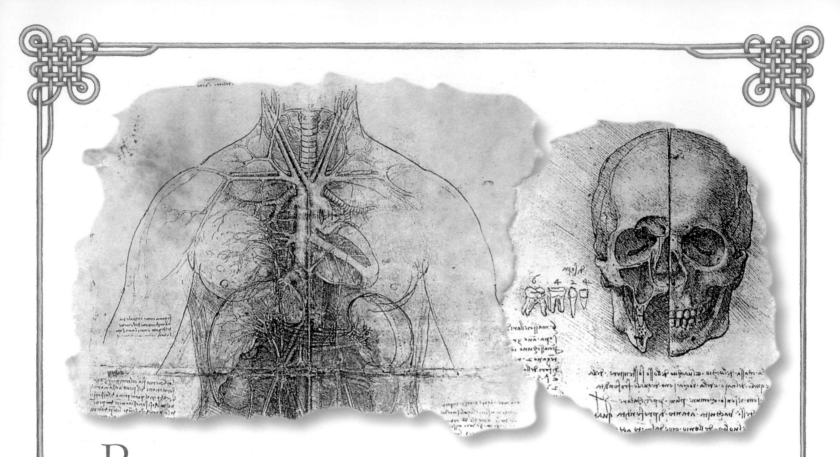

Perhaps the most stunning drawings in Leonardo's notebooks are those that show his careful study of anatomy. During the Renaissance painters often studied the human body so they could learn to draw it correctly. Leonardo did this too. But soon his interest had grown far beyond his work as an artist. He approached anatomy as a scientist. Over a period of twenty-five years he dissected some thirty bodies, making almost two hundred painstaking drawings of them. Besides that, he dissected bears, cows, monkeys, birds, and frogs, comparing their structures to that of humans.

He developed a way of drawing anatomy that medical artists follow to this day. To show the inside of the head, for example, he drew a cross section. To clarify the organs in the abdomen, which lie on top of one another, he drew the ones in front as if they were transparent. And he often drew features from several different views, as if he were turning them in his hand.

It is hard to imagine the fastidious Leonardo doing such work. "If you have a love for this," he wrote, "you may be turned from it by disgust in your stomach; and if that does not deter you, you may be afraid to stay up at night in the company of corpses cut to pieces and lacerated and horrible to behold." Not to mention the fact that the bodies began to decompose before he could finish examining and drawing them. Yet for Leonardo the human body was a wondrous thing. Though he was not a religious man, he wrote that the more he studied the body, the more he was struck by thoughts of God, "who creates nothing superfluous or imperfect."

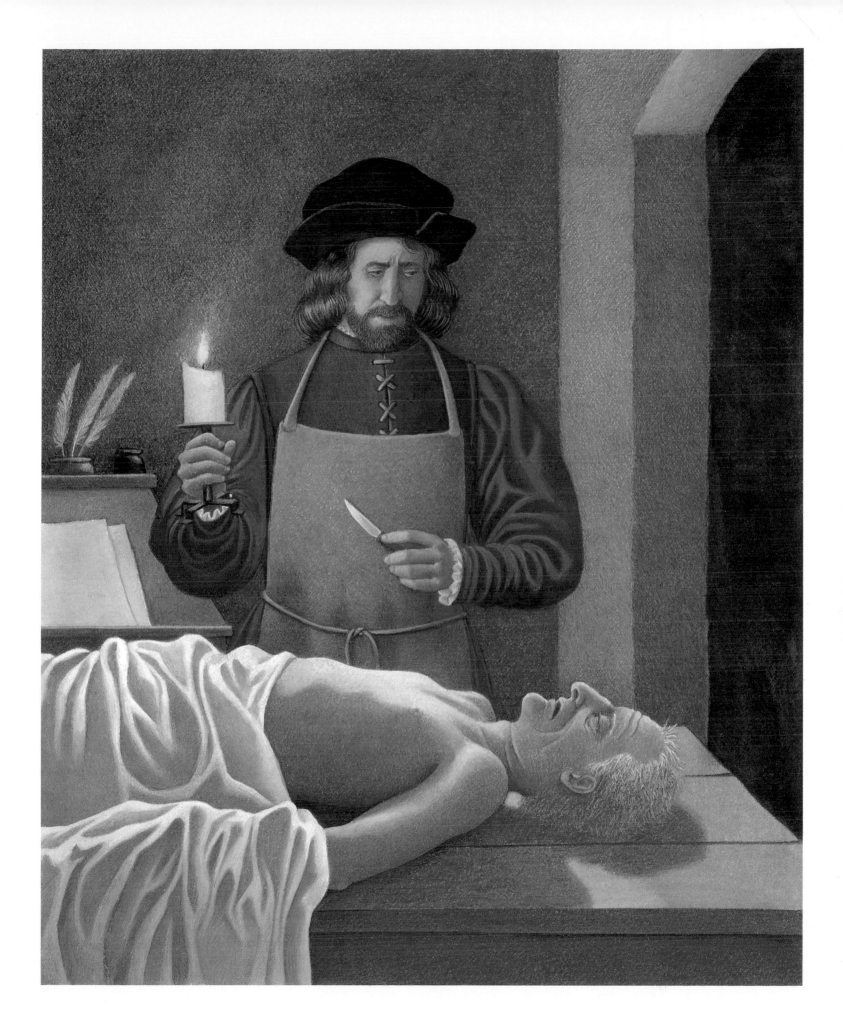

All nature fascinated Leonardo. His notebooks are filled with descriptions of his extraordinary scientific studies. Based on this evidence, he has been called the first modern scientist. In those days people answered questions by looking them up in the Bible or in the writings of the ancient Greeks. Leonardo said that people who did that were using their memories, not their minds. Instead he followed what today we call the scientific method.

First he observed things carefully—the movement of water, the arrangement of leaves on a stem, the flight of birds. That led him to ask questions. Why does a pot lid jump up and down when water starts to boil? Water must expand when it turns to steam, he decided. In attempting to explain what he observed Leonardo was making a hypothesis. But then he had to prove it, and often he wasn't satisfied until he had also measured it. So he set up an experiment. He made a glass cylinder and put water and a piston inside. Then he measured how far the piston rose when the water was heated to boiling. Leonardo was so keen on measuring things that he invented all sorts of devices for that purpose—to measure humidity, altitude, distance traveled, angle of inclination, the speed of wind and water, and the intensity of light.

He often made astonishing mental leaps. When he threw a pebble into a pond, he noticed that circular waves formed around it, expanding steadily outward. From this it occurred to him that sound and light must also travel in waves through the air. What's more, he remembered that he always saw lightning before he heard thunder. He therefore concluded that light waves must travel faster than sound waves.

He trusted his own observations, even if others disagreed with him. For example, up in the mountains he saw fossils of shells, fish, and coral. How had they gotten there? The popular theory of the time was that they had floated up during the great biblical Flood. But Leonardo knew that shells were heavy and did not float. It seemed clear to him that the rock that now formed a mountain once lay at the bottom of the sea. Today we know that in this—as in so many other things—he was correct and far ahead of his time.

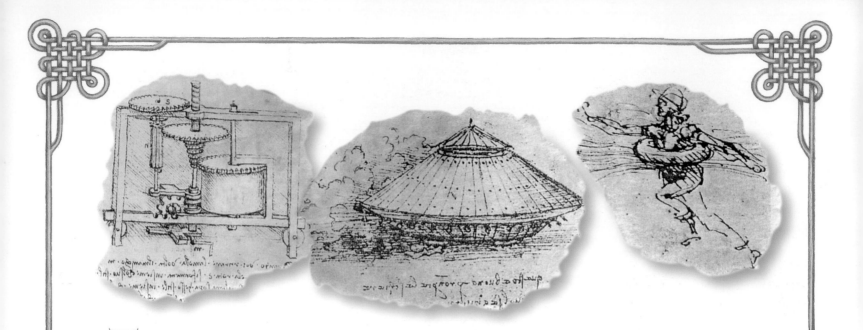

Today, when people talk about Leonardo's notebooks, they probably think first about his inventions. Some writers have given him credit for inventing everything from the submarine to the airplane. As it turns out, while many of his machines and ideas were completely original, others had been thought of before and Leonardo merely improved them. But that should not take away from his reputation as a mechanical genius.

Among Leonardo's many inventions were an underwater diving apparatus, an automatic paper feeder for a printing press, a machine to make metal screws, one of the world's first air-cooling systems, a door that closed automatically, a posthole digger, ski-like shoes for walking on water, an automatic roasting spit, a clock that measured minutes as well as hours, and a spring-powered car. He invented earth-moving machines, a rolling mill for making sheet iron, a device that projected an enlarged image onto a screen, a submarine, pliers, a modern-style monkey wrench, an automated one-man band, and a self-closing toilet lid. He came up with the idea for the contact lens and for prefabricated houses, and he devised formulas for making artificial amber, pearls, and "plastic glass."

If you look at his fearsome war machines, you would hardly imagine that Leonardo was really a man of peace. He loved animals so much that he eventually became a vegetarian and was said to buy birds in the market just to set them free. And yet this gentle man invented, among many other weapons, three different models of machine guns, grenades that threw shrapnel, a very modern-looking bomb, and a steam-powered gun. He improved on an old idea to create an armored car with a complex motor and cannons pointing in every direction. More than four hundred years later, with the addition of a modern engine and caterpillar treads, it was called a tank and became an important weapon in the First World War.

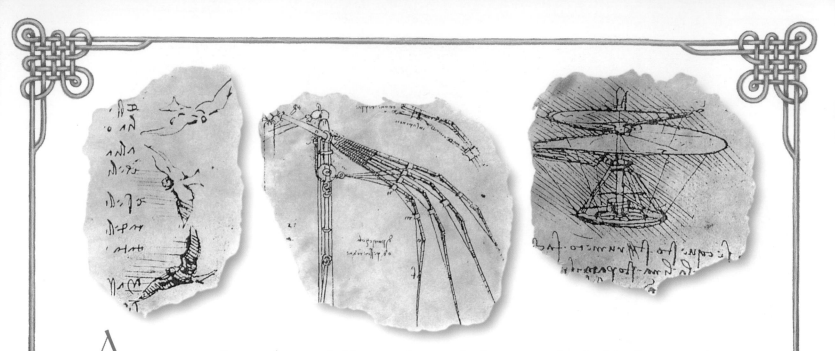

As an inventor, Leonardo is probably most famous for having tried to build a flying machine. He was convinced that "the bird is an instrument functioning according to mathematical laws, and man has the power to reproduce an instrument like this with all its movements." So he analyzed the flight patterns of birds and bats, studied the anatomy of their wings, and observed air currents.

He sketched a variety of designs and finally, after years of preparation, built a model in a secret upstairs room at his workshop. On January 2, 1496, he wrote in his notebook, "Tomorrow morning, I shall make the strap and the attempt." Either he lost his nerve or it didn't work. At any rate, we have no record of it. But the next time he wrote of trying to fly, he was more cautious. "You will experiment with this machine over a lake," he wrote to himself, "and you will wear attached to your belt a long wineskin...so that if you fall in, you will not be drowned."

In 1503 he felt certain of success. Twice he wrote about it in his notebook, speculating grandly that the flight would dumbfound the universe and bring him eternal glory. Yet after years of work and study, Leonardo failed. We don't know any of the details, but much later the son of one of Leonardo's friends wrote these words about the attempt: "Vinci tried in vain."

At least he finally understood the problem. Birds are designed to fly—half the weight of their bodies is in the muscles of flight. Humans, on the other hand, with less than a quarter of their body weight in the arm and chest muscles, would never have the strength to fly like birds.

As a casual afterthought he designed a parachute as well as an airscrew, based on a toy, which some call the first helicopter. He also sketched the pattern of a leaf drifting to earth and under it showed a man on a winglike glider. If he had only worked along these lines instead of trying to imitate the flapping motion of birds, he might have been the first man to fly.

Ten years before coming to Milan, Leonardo had heard rumors of a great bronze statue that was being planned there. It would show Francesco Sforza, father of Ludovico the Moor, mounted on horseback. Such a noble project was sure to bring immortal fame to the man who created it. Leonardo certainly had it in mind when he headed north to Milan. In fact, he specifically mentioned it toward the end of his famous letter to the Moor.

Leonardo worked on this project, off and on, for sixteen years. He began with the horse, planning to make the rider separately and add it later. Leonardo filled his notebooks with beautiful drawings of horses, sketching the finest specimens in the duke's stable. He measured them and worked out ideal proportions. He even dissected horses. Then he began to plan the statue.

Leonardo decided to make it four times life-size. The horse alone would be twenty-four feet high. No one in history had ever cast a sculpture of that size. If he succeeded, it would become one of the wonders of the world. To add to the technical problems, he wanted to show the horse prancing, front legs upraised. Apparently the Moor talked him out of this impractical idea.

In 1493, after ten years of work, Leonardo's full-size clay model was displayed for the admiring public of Milan. All agreed it was a masterpiece. But the hardest part still lay ahead—the casting. Naturally Leonardo studied all the problems that might be involved. He was especially worried about getting all that molten bronze into the mold quickly so that it would not crack as it cooled. He invented a new method for doing this, using four different furnaces. At last the molds were complete and more than seventy tons of bronze gathered. Then, when everything was ready—the Moor used the bronze to make cannons instead!

So the great horse was never cast. And when the French captured Milan in 1499, soldiers used Leonardo's model for target practice. In the end it crumbled and was lost forever.

While Leonardo was still at work on the horse, the Moor gave him another commission. It was to paint a fresco in the monks' dining hall at a nearby church, Santa Maria delle Grazie.

Fresco was a technique used for painting on walls. Water-based paint was applied directly to the plaster while it was still wet. The painter laid down only as much plaster as he could cover in a day, and he had to work quickly, before it dried. Leonardo simply could not paint this way. He needed time to consider. He wanted to go back weeks, months, or even years later and add a little something. So he decided to lay a surface on the wall that would allow him to work as he usually did. It was an experimental method, and tragically it failed. Not long after he had finished, chips of paint began flaking off the wall.

The painting was called *The Last Supper*. Since it was to be in the monks' dining hall, Leonardo made it look as though Jesus and his disciples were eating right there with them. The table at which the disciples sat was just like the ones the monks used. So were the dishes and the glassware and even the tablecloth, with its blue embroidery and fringed ends.

He chose to paint the moment when Jesus had just told his friends that one of them would soon betray him. The disciples were shown reacting in individual ways, with gestures and facial expressions that were very theatrical and full of emotion. Such dramatic intensity had never been achieved in painting before. Leonardo was continuing to invent Renaissance art.

In Milan Leonardo had found a patron and had come to fame as an artist. But after seventeen years, the time came once again to leave. On October 6, 1499, French troops entered the city. The Moor escaped but was later captured and taken to France, where he remained a prisoner until his death eight years later. Leonardo wrote, "The duke lost his states, his personal fortune, and his freedom; none of his projects came to fruition." In December of that year, with the century about to end, Leonardo left Milan.

For the next sixteen years he wandered from place to place, always searching for a reliable patron. He traveled to Mantua, to Venice, then back to Florence. He returned to Milan to work under the French and went to Rome to serve the pope. He even wrote to the sultan of Turkey, offering to design a great bridge for him. But the most unlikely patron he ever had was the bloodthirsty Cesare Borgia.

Borgia was a brilliant general, notorious for his ruthless crimes. His aim was to conquer central Italy, and his means included treachery and murder. For a year Leonardo traveled with Borgia's army as a military engineer, inspecting fortresses and making maps. Along the way he met a young Florentine diplomat, Niccolò Machiavelli. Machiavelli seemed to be making a study of Cesare Borgia. Years later he wrote a book called *The Prince.* It was about power and the most effective way to use it. *The Prince* shocked people because it did not moralize. In fact, it said that a great leader often had to do unspeakable things to accomplish worthwhile goals. Put more simply, the ends justify the means. When the book was published, in 1532, it was condemned by the pope. But others admired it and still do to this day. Napoleon called it "the only book worth reading."

When Leonardo left Borgia's service, his friend Machiavelli did him a great favor. Since he was now chancellor of the Florentine Republic, he was able to get Leonardo an important commission. It was to decorate the Great Council Chamber at the Palazzo della Signoria with a mural of the Battle of Anghiari, a Florentine victory of sixty years before. But to his dismay Leonardo learned that his painting would not be the only one in the room. There would also be one of the Battle of Cascina, to be painted by the rising young artist Michelangelo Buonarroti.

The two men disliked each other. Michelangelo, best known as a sculptor, had received much attention for the remarkable *David* he had carved out of marble. Leonardo resentfully described the art of sculpture as a "mechanical exercise." It was "often accompanied with much sweat and this combines with the dust and turns into a crust of dirt.... [The sculptor's] lodgings are dirty and filled with stone splinters and dust. In the case of the painter," he added, "he sits at great ease...well dressed, moving a light brush with agreeable colors.... His dwelling is clean and filled with beautiful paintings. He often has himself accompanied with music...which he may hear with great pleasure, undisturbed by the pounding of hammers."

For his part, the quarrelsome Michelangelo had once insulted Leonardo in public. "You made a model of a horse you could never cast in bronze," he said, "and which you gave up, to your shame. And the stupid people of Milan had faith in you!"

So the battle of the artists began.

Each planned a picture that allowed him to do what he did best. Michelangelo showed his soldiers surprised while bathing in a stream, because he excelled at the human figure. Leonardo's picture featured horses and was full of violent motion.

Once Leonardo had finished the central section of his cartoon, he began moving his equipment into the chamber. He set up his special scaffold, which he had designed to move easily up and down so that he could reach various parts of the wall. Then he began to prepare the surface for painting. As before, he refused to work in fresco. But this time he had found a recipe for a special technique that would allow him to paint on the wall with oils. He tested it in his workroom and found that the heat of a coal fire dried the paint perfectly.

His cartoon was transferred to the wall, and Leonardo began to paint. But it soon became horribly clear that what had worked on a small scale was not working at all on such a large painting. The fire either was not hot enough or was just too far away. At any rate, the top part of the painting was darkened by the smoke and the rest began to run. Completely discouraged, Leonardo gave up. No amount of pleading or threatening could compel him to come back and repair the mess. *The Battle of Anghiari* stayed just as he left it for sixty years, during which time several artists made copies of it. Eventually it was painted over.

As for Michelangelo, he didn't do his painting either. Having finished only part of his cartoon, he left for Rome to work for the pope.

At about this time, Leonardo's father died, at the age of seventy-eight. Ser Piero had gone on to marry two more times. Unlike his first two marriages, these were blessed with children. In fact, at his death he left behind thirteen children, and the youngest was only six.

Ser Piero did not leave a will, so the reasonable thing was to divide the inheritance evenly among the thirteen children. But Leonardo's half brothers and sisters were a greedy lot. Under the leadership of one of the brothers, Ser Giuliano, they went to court to deprive Leonardo of his portion, on the ground that he was illegitimate.

Three years later Uncle Francesco died too. He had always loved his oldest nephew and must have been shocked by the cruel way he was being treated. So Francesco made sure to leave a will, and in it he gave everything he owned to Leonardo.

Once again Ser Giuliano went to court, this time to challenge Francesco's will. After a long and painful wait the court gave Leonardo the use of Francesco's land and money, but only during his lifetime. At his death everything would go to his half brothers and sisters.

It was a bitter time. Leonardo was growing old, and his health was failing. Though he lived in splendid surroundings in both Milan and Rome, he had no wife or children to comfort him. The struggle over the inheritance had broken his spirit. Wandering from place to place he had no roots, no true home. All anyone seemed to want from him was pictures. And though he continued to work on occasion, Leonardo had not been interested in painting for a long time. It was said that he was "weary of the paintbrush." The pope was annoyed with him, complaining that Leonardo would "never finish anything." All around him new young artists were doing great work and getting praised for it. It seemed that Leonardo was out of fashion.

At this pitiful time in Leonardo's life he was rescued by his last and most sympathetic patron. The king of France, Francis I, offered him the title Premier Painter and Engineer and Architect of the King. He would be well paid. And his new home would be the charming manor house of Cloux, near the royal château at Amboise. All the king expected in return was Leonardo's conversation.

Sometime in 1516 or 1517 Leonardo left Italy for France. He took with him two young men who had entered his life as apprentices but whom he loved as if they were his sons. The first had come to live with Leonardo twenty-five years before, in Milan. The boy was ten years old at the time, and his antics both charmed and horrified his master. After Leonardo took his young pupil to a friend's house for dinner he wrote that the boy "behaved badly at table, supped for two and did mischief for four, broke three bottles, and knocked over the wine." Worse, he often stole things and then lied about it. Leonardo renamed his little pupil Salai, a Tuscan word for "little devil."

The second pupil was Francesco Melzi, a handsome young aristocrat who had been with Leonardo for ten years. Unlike the knavish Salai, Melzi was gentle and refined, a source of comfort and protection for Leonardo in his last years. It is possible that Salai became jealous of Melzi. For whatever reason, he eventually left France and went back to Milan. Melzi stayed on at Leonardo's side for as long as he lived.

After the long journey Leonardo and his party were glad to settle down in their new home. Almost every day the king came to see him. Often he brought a topic for discussion, such as "Tell me about the soul." The answers must have delighted the king, for he later said that he "did not believe that there had ever been another man born into the world who knew as much as Leonardo." He was, the king said, "a very great philosopher."

Leonardo had brought with him his notebooks and three paintings. One was an odd picture of St. John the Baptist. Another was the *Virgin and Child with St. Anne* (which was almost finished but not quite). The last, a portrait of "a certain Florentine lady," is probably the most famous painting in the world. Called in Europe *La Gioconda,* we know it as the *Mona Lisa.*

The picture originally showed a woman sitting on a balcony, flanked by two pillars. At some time over the years the pillars were cut off, but you can still see their bases and the ledge. No one knows for sure who actually sat for the portrait, though tradition has it that she was the third wife of a wealthy Florentine silk merchant. But it doesn't really matter. The *Mona Lisa* shows us everything that Leonardo thought was important in painting.

Although he was painting on a flat surface, he created the illusion of three dimensions by a technique called *chiaroscuro*—the masterful use of light and deep shadow. Such realism was a new achievement in the history of art, and Leonardo called it "the soul of painting." But he wanted his pictures to be more than visually real. They should seem to have movement as well. One of the ways he achieved this is called *contrapposto.* This means that his figures were never stiff and straight. They curved and twisted, with the head usually turned in a different direction from the torso. To these techniques he added a third ingredient, which he put into everything he set his hand (or mind) to. That ingredient is genius.

It is lovely to imagine Leonardo in his last years, living in comfort, surrounded by friends, displaying his incredible accomplishments to worshipful admirers. And it would complete the picture to believe the story of his death as told by Vasari in *The Lives of the Painters*. He wrote that on May 2, 1519, having made his peace with God, the sixty-seven-year-old Leonardo da Vinci died in the arms of the king of France.

And so it was believed until 1850, when a French scholar pointed out a decree of the king that was dated May 3—one day after Leonardo's death. It was signed at a place far from Amboise. Because of this, the scholar concluded that Francis would have been traveling on the day Leonardo died. Obviously the king could not have been at his bedside. Most historians have accepted this theory. But later another scholar looked at the decree more closely and found something interesting. It was signed not by the king himself but by the chancellor in his absence.

So let us leave the king of France where he belongs, at the bedside of his friend. This is how Vasari tells it: "Thereupon he was seized by...the messenger of death;...the King having risen and having taken his head, in order to assist him and show him favor...that he might alleviate his pain, [Leonardo's] spirit, which was divine, knowing that it could not have any greater honor, expired in the arms of the King."

POSTSCRIPT

Leonardo was buried in the chapel of Saint-Florentin at Amboise. Over the next three hundred years the buildings gradually fell into ruin. Then, in 1802, Napoleon ordered that they be restored. Unfortunately the man chosen for the job decided the chapel was not worth saving. It was torn down, and its stones, as well as the tombs and gravestones, were used to restore the château. The lead coffins were melted down, and the bones left in a heap. One of the gardeners had the kindness to bury them.

Years later the common grave was opened, and an attempt was made to decide which of the skeletons was Leonardo's. One was chosen because it was tall and had a fine head. It was later reburied, the grave marked with a plaque that said these *might* be the remains of Leonardo da Vinci. They probably are not.

Leonardo's work suffered a similar fate. Today only about a dozen of his paintings have been identified. Of those, the *Mona Lisa* lost her pillars and a lovely portrait, *Ginevra Benci,* is missing a strip on the bottom containing her hands. Several paintings have disappeared, and others have been badly retouched. *The Battle of Anghiari* is gone, and what we know of it comes only from copies made by other artists. *The Last Supper* seems plagued by misfortune. In 1624 the monks cut a door into the wall, removing Jesus' feet. The painting was twice damaged by floods. And during the Napoleonic Wars the room was used as a stable. Idle soldiers are said to have passed the time by throwing bricks at the apostles' heads. During World War II the chapel was destroyed by Allied bombs. Miraculously the wall bearing *The Last Supper* did not fall, saved by a pile of sandbags.

Leonardo's notebooks went to Francesco Melzi, who took them home to Italy. He tried to organize the thousands of pages of notes and drawings. With the help of two assistants, he selected and copied out all Leonardo's writings on art. Yet for some unknown reason the resulting *Treatise on Painting* was not published until 1651.

After Melzi's death, in 1570, the notebooks were given to his son Orazio, a lawyer, who did not value them at all. He stored them in his attic and then began selling them or even giving them away. Soon they were scattered all over Europe. Some collectors cut them up and pasted them into albums. At least a third of the sheets were lost. Perhaps someone used the priceless pages to line a drawer.

So for three hundred years the public knew Leonardo only as an artist. His lifetime of scientific research and his marvelous inventions bore no fruit because his notebooks remained in the hands of collectors, and few other people knew about them before 1800. It is frustrating to imagine how the development of science and technology might have been advanced if only his work had been published. In just two examples: Leonardo worked out the first law of motion before Newton, and one hundred years before the first telescope was built, while making a study of optics, he wrote a note to himself to "make glasses to see the moon large."

There is still a chance that some of the lost sheets will eventually turn up, as happened in 1965. To everyone's joy and surprise, a collection of notebook pages was found tucked away in the stacks of the National Library in Madrid. How tantalizing it is to think that six thousand pages of Leonardo's notes might still be out there, waiting to reveal their secrets.

BIBLIOGRAPHY

Bramly, Serge. *Leonardo: Discovering the Life of Leonardo da Vinci.* Translated by Sian Reynolds. New York: Harper-Collins, 1991.

Clark, Kenneth. *Leonardo da Vinci.* New York: Viking Penguin, 1988.

Kemp, Martin. *Leonardo da Vinci: The Marvellous Works of Nature and Man.* Cambridge: Harvard University Press, 1981.

Kemp, Martin, and Jane Roberts, exhibition selectors. *Leonardo da Vinci.* Catalog of an exhibition held at the Hayward Gallery, South Bank Centre, London. New Haven: Yale University Press, 1989.

Philipson, Morris, editor. *Leonardo da Vinci: Aspects of the Renaissance Genius.* New York: George Braziller, 1966.

Reti, Ladislao, editor. *The Unknown Leonardo.* New York: Harry N. Abrams, 1990.

Richter, Jean Paul. *The Notebooks of Leonardo da Vinci,* volumes 1 and 2. New York: Dover, 1970.

Santi, Bruno. *Leonardo da Vinci.* Italy: SCALA, Istituto Fotografico, 1990.

Turner, A. Richard. *Inventing Leonardo.* New York: Alfred A. Knopf, 1993.

Vasari, Giorgio. *Lives of the Most Eminent Painters, Sculptors, and Architects.* Translated by Gaston DuC. DeVere. Introduction by Kenneth Clark. New York: Harry N. Abrams, 1979.

Wallace, Robert, and the editors of Time-Life Books. *The World of Leonardo, 1452–1519.* New York: Time, 1966.

RECOMMENDED FOR YOUNGER READERS

Marshall, Norman V. *Leonardo da Vinci.* Illustrated by Aldo Ripamonti. In the series *What Made Them Great.* Englewood Cliffs, N.J.: Silver Burdett, 1981.

McLanathan, Richard. *Leonardo da Vinci.* New York: Harry N. Abrams, 1990.

Mühlberger, Richard. *What Makes a Leonardo a Leonardo?* New York: Viking/The Metropolitan Museum of Art, 1994.

Pierre, Michel. *The Renaissance.* Translated by Nan Buranelli. Morristown, N.J.: Silver Burdett, 1987.

Provensen, Alice, and Martin Provensen. *Leonardo da Vinci.* New York: Viking, 1984.

Skira-Venturi, Rosabianca. *A Weekend with Leonardo da Vinci.* Translated by Ann Keay Beneduce. New York: Rizzoli, 1993.